TABLE *talk*
FAMILY DINNER DEVOS

DANIELLE MACAULAY

Copyright © 2017 Danielle Macaulay

0-692-89321-0
978-0-692-89321-0

ACKNOWLEDGMENTS

Thank you to Pam Farrel, for encouraging me to run with the idea of this book, and to Bill Farrel, for believing in me as a writer, and helping me hone my writing skill.

Thank you to Ruth Anaya and my mother, Judy Bodaly, for skillfully and carefully editing this project.

Thank you to my friend and mentor Tara, for praying, listening, encouraging and teaching me. I am the wife, mom and cook that I am today because of your example.

Thank you to my husband, Dan for being a support and confidence builder along this writing journey, and for *all* the hours of techie and graphic help. This project would still just be a Word document if it wasn't for you. You're the best!

And, thank you to Keaton and Braden, for giving me the best material for this book. You always keep me smiling. I love you both SO much!

DEDICATION:

To my boys. I love you more.

PREFACE

Parents, do you remember that old show, "Kids say the darnedest things"? It always gave us a good chuckle. I'm sure that you would agree that kids are often cute, funny, and sometimes even have something profound to say. Most of the time, this is unbeknownst to them, which makes it even more adorable.

Dinner time is often when kids can be the *least* adorable. It can be frustrating and downright exhausting to get the little tikes to eat their greens and keep them from spilling their milk. I am hoping that this book, which is filled with some funny things our kids have said, will take away the dinner time blues and add some fun to the occasion, so you will all want to keep congregating around the table.

Studies show that families who eat together, stick together. Doing dinner together means building closer relationships and nurturing a sense of belonging. It helps young children develop a sense of security and older children achieve better grades. Children will be happier and less stressed. And they may very well be more prone to eat their fruits and veggies! The dinner table is the perfect environment where children can learn valuable life skills such as problem solving and engaging in conversation. Hopefully, this book will help you weave God into the conversation as well, because learning to serve Him is the most valuable life lesson of all!

We truly believe that the Lord has given us each other – husband, wife, and our children – in order to make us more like Christ and faithful followers of The Lord. That is our ultimate goal. Mom, dad, sis and bro...we all need to become more like Jesus – all the while growing closer together and nearer to God. We hope that you create some hilarious and loving family memories around your dinner table, and together learn some valuable life lessons. Most of all, we want your declaration to be:

"As for me and my house, we will serve The Lord." (Joshua 24:15)

So, pull up a seat, pass the potatoes, and dig in to this dinner devotional while you dig into your food! You'll be nourished, body and soul!

Love,
~ The Macaulays

CAUSE AND EFFECT

> "When I eat boogers,
> I get a cough."
> – Braden, age 2

I'll admit it – I hate January, February, and March. They are the gloomiest months where we live, and the time of year when it seems we get our turn at having a cold or catching the flu. So my family eats lots of fruits and veggies, remembers their vitamins, washes their hands, and gets a good night's rest, hoping to decrease the chance of us getting sick.

I'm talking about "cause and effect". Have you heard of the phrase? "Cause and effect" is when one event is a result of another. You know – like, if you drop a hammer on your toe, you will develop a throbbing, painful pinky. Here are a few other examples:

Cause: He never brushes his teeth
Effect: He has 5 cavities.

Cause: A basketball player travels during a game
Effect: The referee calls a penalty.

Cause: You flip the light switch on
Effect: The room lights up.

Even little Braden figured out the law of cause and effect, and he unashamedly shared his thought process for getting sick. There we were, at the doctor's office on a frigid February morning. As the doc listened closely to his chest with the stethoscope, Braden fessed up: "When I eat boogers, I get a cough".We all cracked up a little, and the doc agreed with Braden, and told him he might want to stop eating boogers and try eating more broccoli instead.

The biblical idea of "cause and effect" is called "sowing and reaping". Farmers know this term well. In farming, sowing is what gets planted, and reaping is what is later harvested. If you plant corn seed, a corn stalk grows, not green beans! In the same way, if we plant seeds of laziness, we won't have much to show for time we wasted. God is reminding us that whatever we do, there will be a consequence – good or bad! And Braden is reminding us of the same!

GET 'EM TALKING:

• Parents: Share with your kids a time when you "reaped what you sowed" in a negative way, and another time in a positive way.

SOUL FOOD:

• Galatians 6:7-10
• 2 Corinthians 9:6-8
• Proverbs 11:18
• Hosea 10:12-13

PROUD HOT DOG

"Mom, you're like a hot dog,
because you're hot!
... and because you're a dog."
– Keaton, age 4

Have you ever felt very proud about something? Maybe you've been proud of a mark on your test, hitting that home run, or proud of a new cool outfit you're wearing. Or, mom and dad, maybe you're proud of your home or your job. I'm CERTAIN you are super proud of those kiddos that are also driving you nuts around the table right now. It's ok to be proud – but not *too* proud. Things get dangerous when we start to forget that GOD is the one who gave us abilities, opportunities, and talents. (Look up what happened to King Uzziah in 2 Chronicles 26:16-23! Yikes!) Parents, thankfully God gives us some reality checks through our children. Our kiddos have a way of keeping us humble, don't they? They're the first to tell us when our breath stinks, our arms are flabby, or our singing is off key (sorry, Mom!) Let me tell you of a time the kid in our life gave me a reality check.

We were sitting around the dining table, like you may be doing right now. Hot dogs were the "gourmet" choice of the night. As we were eating, a light bulb went off in Keaton's little mind, while scarfing down his dinner: "Mom! You're like a hot dog, because you're HOT!" My face lit up and I gave him a big grin, with an "awww". Such a smart little fellow he was! Well, I wish he had of stopped right there. Just as my pride began to swell, he popped my ballooned head with the second part of his thought: "and because you're a DOG!" I heard belly laughs rise up to the left of me – a very amused dad. My brow furrowed. Well, so much for that. Truth is, our adorable little Keaton had no idea what he was saying. But we sure did, and, it was pretty funny. This isn't the only time he's pulled the rug of pride right out from underneath me. He's lucky he's so darn cute!

Get 'em Talking:

- Have everyone take a turn at saying an ability, characteristic, resource or talent they have that they like about themselves. Discuss how GOD has blessed you with those things and what would happen if God was taken out of the equation.

- Read this scripture aloud: "Every good and perfect gift comes down from the father of lights." James 1:17

Soul Food:

- Proverbs 11:2
- James 4:6
- Philippians 2:3
- 1 Corinthians 13:4

HIDE AND SEEK

"So, THAT'S where God has
been hiding all this time...
In a burning bush!"
— Keaton, age 4

Nana and Papa gave Keaton a Children's Bible when he
was a baby. As I read through it with him, I realized that
there are so many stories in the Bible that even
blockbuster films have been challenged to keep up with.
Plagues of frogs, boils, locusts, and rivers turning to
blood. Every animal that exists being packed onto a big
boat during a world storm. And a pip squeak of a kid
killing a giant of a man with a stone! These stories are all
mind-blowing; and they all REALLY HAPPENED! David and
Goliath was certainly a favorite of ours to act out, with
our costume helmets and swords, some extra wrestling
moves added in for fun, and a soft couch to land on when
there was a final kerplunk. It is fun to make the stories of
the Bible come alive.

One particular day when we were reading about God
appearing to Moses in a burning bush, Keaton had an
epiphany: "OH! So THAT'S where He's been hiding all this
time – in a burning bush!" I chuckled to myself, but then
clued in that all this time, Keaton had been learning
about God but he was confused as to where God was. He
hadn't actually seen Him with his own eyes yet. This story

seemed to explain things though. Keaton assumed God had been hiding in that fiery bush the whole time.

This was a funny and cute little moment, but also a moment that I was able to teach Keaton that even though we can't see God with our own eyes, He is right here with us. I was glad that he had been wondering where God was, because even though he didn't find Him hiding in our back bushes, he still found Him...because we had been searching, by reading God's word. It takes having eyes of faith to see God – not having 20/20 vision. God says that when we believe He is real and when we look for Him, we will find Him. So, let's be like Moses, when he said "This is amazing!... I must go see (God)!" (Exodus 3:3)

GET 'EM TALKING:

- Take turns telling everyone what your favorite story in the Bible is, and why.

- What are some ways we can build our faith and "find" God?" (Hint: Psalm 19:1 is a great way!)

- Have someone read this verse aloud: "You will seek me and you will find me when you seek me with all of your heart." Jeremiah 29:13

SOUL FOOD:

- Psalm 19:1
- 1 Chronicles 16:11
- Psalm 14:2
- Hebrews 11:6

MIRACLE MAN

> "I can do miracles too.
> I can turn food into poop!"
> – Keaton, age 3

Sorry mom and dad, but a portion of this dinner devo might not be the most polite table talk. I'll try to get it over with right off the bat. (Kids, try not to giggle *too* much!) So, we all know that "potty" conversation is heightened during potty training, right? Pee and poop and things like that become normal conversation, even when it comes to learning about Jesus...at least, at *our* house it was.

We were sitting and waiting, waiting and sitting. The toilet paper was squeezed tightly in his fist. We knew it was imminent. Keaton had to go "potty". Well, I know it's dinner time, so I won't go into any more detail, other than he was successful – and very happy about it. This was his declaration: "I can do miracles too! I can turn food into poop!!"

I remembered that the Sunday prior, he had learned about the miracle of Jesus turning water into wine. I'll admit that I laughed real hard at his declaration. The kid thought he was a miracle maker. I obliged him and said, "Yes, it's a miracle!" As moms would know, it really *is* a miracle when they learn to use the potty! Now, we all really know that going to the bathroom is a normal part of human life. But then, why is it SO funny to all you boys!!??

What makes something a miracle? It is a miracle ONLY when God alone can make something happen! Miracles are also called wonders, marvels, extraordinary events, a mystery, and a supernatural phenomenon. The Bible tells us that it is GOD who is that marvelous mystery who does extraordinary things! From the creation of this world to the birth of a baby in Bethlehem, to healing a blind man with some mud, and saving us from our sins...ONLY GOD can do such miraculous things! He's the only miracle man around here!

GET 'EM TALKING:

• Read this verse aloud: "You are the God who performs miracles; you display your power among the peoples." Psalm 77:14

• Jesus' first miracle while he was on this earth was turning water into wine at a wedding, so that his glory would be revealed and his disciples would have faith to believe. Brainstorm all of the miracles that you can think of recorded in the Bible. God performs miracles of protection, healing, judgment, and all of them should build our faith in our all-powerful God!

• Now that you've talked about miracles recorded in the Bible, take turns going around the table and talk about a miracle God has done for YOU! (Hey, moms: If it's that your little

6

GOD KNOWS WHAT FLOATS YOUR BOAT

> "God, I really, really, really, really, really want to win at wrestling!"
> – Braden, age 3

Our Braden is something fierce! We often call him "Braden the Destroyer". He enjoys anything that involves physical force: knocking down Lego towers, football tackles, head butts, body slams, and everything in between. One of the boy's favorite after dinner family time activities is wrestling. This usually involves their dad whipping pillows at them, throwing them on the couch, and lots of tickling. They return the gestures with pushes, punches, and karate chops, and as much physical force as they can muster. I think dad only has a few more years before they can completely overtake him.

As the only female in the house, I try to keep up. Yes, I have been known to let them jump on me while I'm under a tower of cushions, but a lot of the time I simply have to leave the room and go do some dishes. Wrestling time always is full of laughter...until it ends with crying. And that's too much for this momma to handle! But, the boys love it, especially Braden. I haven't seen his face light up more than when his dad let's him rock 'em and sock 'em and haul off and give a big blow to the gut. Of course they have some guidelines. They know that this type of stuff happens only with daddy, and when he lets them. I've joked before that wrestling is Braden's love language. But that certainly is true because after some vigorous tumbling on the floor with dad and big bro, Braden is very happy and affectionate and dives in for a cuddle.

The very first time that Braden initiated prayer at bedtime, his prayer was that God would help him beat the big boys the next time they wrestled. God knows Braden. He made Braden a rough and tumble kind of kid. God also knows what Braden loves because He created him to enjoy those things. God knows the things that you love too, and He wants to give you those things, as long as they line up with His rules. God says that He loves to give us the desires of our heart when we delight in Him first. God hears your every prayer, big or little, silly or significant. He wants you to ask Him!

GET 'EM TALKING:

- What floats *your* boat? Go around the table, youngest to oldest, and say two or three things that you love to do. How could you do those things to love God and love others?

SOUL FOOD:
- Psalm 37:4-5

ONE BODY, MANY PARTS

"Mom, you're a good cooker.
...and dad, you're a good eater!"
– Keaton, age 3

We are all created with unique talents and abilities. You may be really great athletically, while your sister stinks at catching a ball. BUT, your sis may be able to sing circles around you – and that's ok! God often puts people together who need each other. Over the years, our diverse capabilities have become very clear to us. God needs us all to work together to achieve great things. Don't get frustrated when someone may shine in an area that makes you fall flat on your face. Encourage that person to shine for Jesus while they do what they were created to do! And, YOU – to the best of your ability – do what you were created for. Watch how God will fulfill you, all the while blessing others.

We all need some encouragement now and again. Make sure that you are the one to get the ball rolling. When you see someone using their gifts for God, let them know! And, when you notice someone who might be discouraged, look for positive things in them, and tell them. Build them up. I am so glad that Keaton pointed out that he likes my cooking, and also how great his dad is at devouring my meals.

You can do more than just skating or sketching, dancing or diving. Did you know that God has given every one of you sitting around your table a spiritual gift as well? The Bible lists the spiritual gifts in 1 Corinthians 12. They are all given so that we can help each other out. As you do everything to the best of your ability, you will not only please your parents and God, but you'll also be helping other people in the process! You'll feel really great too. Cool, isn't it!?

GET 'EM TALKING:

- Read the list of spiritual gifts aloud, and then go around the table and share what you think your spiritual gift might be. Then, encourage another member of your family by sharing what talent you can see God has gifted them with.

SOUL FOOD:

- 1 Corinthians 12:7-11
- Romans 12:6-8
- 1 Peter 4:10-11

DON'T EAT "DERMS"!

"I'm eating derms."

– Keaton, age 3

It was a hot, sticky summer night in Connecticut. We decided to make an impromptu trip to the local ice cream shop. When one of us suggests ice cream, it doesn't take much arm twisting. Once we were in possession of our gigantic cones, we plunked down on the curb outside of the shop, chit chatted, watched cars zoom by and enjoyed our treats. Dad and mom took turns "helping" Keaton with the drips of ice cream he couldn't keep up with. Ice cream drips were racing down his cone, onto his arms, and into his lap. Like I said, it was hot! As Dan and I gabbed a bit more with each other, we were distracted and didn't pay attention to our three-year-old for a second.

When we turned our heads to check on him again, we found him a few feet over. To our horror, he was licking some dripped ice cream off of the GARBAGE CAN! As you can imagine, we grabbed that toddler and asked him, "WHAT are you doing!!?" Keaton's matter-of-fact answer was, "I'm eating derms." (Translation: I'm eating GERMS). "You've got that right!", I replied.

Well, many years later I can laugh at that one, but at the time we sure were horrified! We knew toddlers can be gross, but LICKING a public garbage can took 'gross' up a couple notches! (insert gag reflex)

I'm pretty certain that most of us who are older than three years of age would refrain from licking garbage cans, no matter WHAT is on them. That's just downright gross. But, if we think about it, often we can be tempted to do really silly, wrong, or just plain nasty things, because they seem desirable at the time. Keaton didn't seem to mind one bit that his tongue would come into contact with the surface of a garbage can – something crawling with "DERMS" – if it meant he'd have a few more licks of that yummy, irresistible ice cream. But even at three, he knew that he'd be ingesting something bad. But still, he was willing to take that risk if it meant having something he wanted. Thankfully, Keaton did not get sick from the germs, but who knows about next time? Keep this story in mind the next time you're faced with a sticky situation. Is it worth it to risk consuming bad things, just to get something you want?

GET 'EM TALKING:

- Discuss some things that look tempting but might not be that good for you. For example, watching a really cool and funny movie that also has rude, inappropriate, or curse words in it.

- Have one family member read this Bible verse aloud: "Run from anything that stimulates youthful lusts. Instead, pursue righteous living, faithfulness, love and peace. Enjoy the companionship of those who

call on the Lord with pure
hearts." 2 Timothy 2:22

Soul Food:

- Proverbs 14:12
- James 1:13-16

11

TO EAT THE FRUIT OR NOT TO EAT THE FRUIT

> "NOW I get why they don't let
> fruit across the border!"
>
> – Keaton, age 8

Our good friend, comedian, Leland Klassen, does a comedy routine all about crossing the Canadian/American border. He reminds us of the good old days, when the Americans loved their "neighbors to the North" and the "biggest threat" from Canadians going into America was the fruit they might be carrying. My kids LOVE hearing Leland perform that one story. Their favorite part is Leland acting out a man driving up to the border and yelling to his wife, "Eat the fruit, Lois! EAT THE FRUIT!". As Canadians living in America, we must always remember to "EAT THE FRUIT" before we make our way to the border.

One morning, as I was discussing sin with Keaton, I reminded him about the story of Adam and Eve. He then exclaimed, "NOW I get why they don't let fruit across the border!!" I could almost see the light bulb turning on above his adorable little noggin. It was as if he never quite understood why the apple was a bad thing. That was my fault. I had always encouraged him to eat as much fruit as possible, but had never taken the time to explain that along with the good things that fruit has to offer, it can also be a carrier of disease, and the government doesn't want disease to spread into their country. I now had the chance to do some explaining.

Yes, fruit is a very good thing – my personal favorite is pineapple! – but God told Adam and Eve NOT to eat it from a certain tree. We may never know exactly why He forbid them, but when loving parents give a rule, we should simply obey, whether we understand their reasons or not. We know how things turned out. They were tempted by Satan (that sneaky serpent) to disobey God and eat the fruit anyway. Adam and Eve gave into the temptation and disobeyed. As a result, they had to pay some serious consequences – and we are STILL paying for it today!

Throughout our life we will be faced with countless temptations (pretty much EVERY day!). There will always be "forbidden" things. Often times, the things that we aren't supposed to do, and the people we shouldn't do them with, seem very desirable - like a crisp and juicy, shiny red apple. But, just because something seems good, doesn't make it good. We need to trust our parents, our pastors and God to lead us in the right direction, even the times we don't understand. God says "I will lead you on the best pathway for your life. I will advise you and watch over you." Aren't you glad that such a big, powerful, wise and capable God is in control? And, aren't you glad that everything He does is because He loves us SO much. When we know who He is and trust Him, it will be easier to say "no" when the enemy tries to tempt us to disobey God - no matter how shiny or how harmless the enemy makes disobedience seem. God always knows when there's a worm inside an apple!

GET 'EM TALKING:

- Parents, share with your kids an occasion where you gave into temptation, and what the result was. Was it helpful or harmful? Was it worth it?

Soul Food:

- Psalms 119:11
- Matthew 26:41
- Ephesians 6:11
- James 1:12
- James 4:7

20/20 VISION

"I'm trying to see Caleb's heart
like Jesus does."

– Keaton, age 6

Do you know someone who is mean and grumpy? Does anyone ever rub you the wrong way and get under your skin? Are there people who have crawled their way onto your VERY LAST NERVE?? The answer to all three of those questions is a whopping YES! We can't control what others do and say, but we certainly have control over how we respond.

I think Keaton hit the nail on the head here, when he told me that he was trying to understand a boy whose actions were bothering him. Keaton just didn't understand, but he understood that Jesus knows all of us better than anyone else. He knows what is going on in our minds and in our hearts. He knows every detail of our lives, and so HE gets why Caleb was acting out. There's a story and a reason behind everything we say and do. How insightful of Keaton to try to imagine how Jesus looks at Caleb. I'm guessing that instantly, he had more grace, compassion, and love for Caleb. I think his frustrations fizzled just a bit too.

Whoa, parents – isn't it mind blowing when our kids teach US!? There have been many times when I've been hurt, annoyed, confused, or frustrated by someone. I certainly

of the Lord, and nothing makes us more joyful than spending time with you, our kids.

Parents, this is my challenge to you: this coming week, be a "yes" parent. Whether it's saying "yes" to one more scoop of ice cream after dinner, one more story at bedtime, or playing some football out in the back yard even though the chores need to be done – say "YES!" I find that a little extra goes a long way. Chances are, that "lightening up" will make *every* member of your family become more joyful, and your kids won't view you as an old "stick in the mud".

GET' EM TALKING:

- I'm kind of a neat freak, but my boys think mud is fun, so I am going to get a little dirty with them, and be ok with it this week. Brainstorm some ways that YOU can all have some extra fun together this week, even if it means getting your boots a little dirty and your house a little messy!

SOUL FOOD:

- Psalm 68:3
- Psalm 118:24
- Proverbs 17:22

PESTERING AND PERSISTING

"Mom, can I please play video games after my school work?"
– Keaton, age 5

"Maybe"

"Can't you just say yes or no?"

"Okay, no"

"Alright, you can say maybe!"

Have you ever had this type of conversation with each other? Kids have a reputation for hounding parents relentlessly for what they want. In the past 24 hours alone, I've been pestered for screen time, a piece of lemon cake that is perched far back out of reach on the counter, for new toy cars, and "just ONE more story" at bedtime. God has given children the gift of persistence when they see something they want, and they know how to win the battle of the wills if us parents don't have unwavering resolve. I'll admit, sometimes I just want to run and hide!

God never hides from us though. I know that it can seem like sometimes your prayers aren't getting through to Him, and He must be snoozing up there. But God welcomes our requests any time of the day. He never tires of hearing our voice. He wants us to trust that He's got everything under control and that He's got our best interest in mind. When it seems like God isn't giving us what we want when we want it, it's not that He doesn't like us or doesn't want to bless us. On the contrary! God loves his kids SO much that sometimes He says "no" because He knows it's for our own good. Just think: if I said "yes" to Keaton's relentless requests to play video games, he'd be a Minecraft playing zombie with zero education. He'd wither away to nothing because he'd forego eating. He'd be lonely because he'd forget about all his friends. So, as you can see, sometimes it's necessary for the ones who take care of you to say "no", even though it doesn't feel good at the time. God is our caregiver, and he cares SO much for us. Keep that in mind when your prayers might not be answered when, or the way, you had hoped.

Some great news is that God WELCOMES our pestering, or shall I say, our persistence! The Bible tells us that the prayers of the righteous, who don't give up asking or praying, can sometimes actually change God's mind! So, if you're praying for the RIGHT things, you may see the results you're looking for! Whether you hear "yes", "no", or "you have to wait a while", always know that God wants to give us good things and protect us from bad things. He knows exactly how and when to answer every one of our requests! I know that you will definitely annoy your parents sometimes, but you will NEVER bug God with your prayers!

GET 'EM TALKING:

- Have a member from your family read this verse aloud: "And we are confident that he hears us whenever we ask for anything that pleases him." 1 John 5:14

- Read the story Jesus told of the "persistent widow" found in Luke 18:1-8. What is the lesson we can learn from the unjust judge?

SOUL FOOD:

- John 15:7
- Psalm 37:4-5
- Isaiah 65:24
- Philippians 4:16
- James 4:3

X-RAY VISION AND OTHER SUPER POWERS

> "Mom, don't look behind my back...
> I don't have anything in my hand."
> — Braden, age 4

If a kid had a cute but severely guilty look on his face, and hands in a tiny fist behind his back, would you believe him if he told you he wasn't hiding anything!? Toddlers can be so innocent, but they can also be quite devious and manipulative - in the most adorable way! I almost always know when Braden is up to no good. His doe-eyed face looking up at me gives it away. Yet, every so often, he pulls a fast one on me. While kids are young, they might believe that mom knows everything – that we have "eyes in the back of our heads", but soon enough kids begin to realize that mom and dad can't always be watching. But you know who DOES see everything? You guessed it. God does. He doesn't just have eyes in the back of His head, He's got eyes EVERYWHERE! God is "omnipresent", which means that He is everywhere. Kind of crazy, right!? It's true, though! He sees through everything we do. X-ray vision is only one of His superpowers. Even though your parents will never know all that you do and say, always remember that God does! You can't hide ANYTHING from Him!

Thankfully, an even cooler superpower that God has is forgiveness. When we make the wrong choice or mess up,

He is gracious to forgive us if we ask Him to. But we must try our best not to do it again. I am so glad that I serve a God who has WAY more superpowers than Batman, Superman, and Wonder Woman combined!!

GET 'EM TALKING:

- Everyone say what super power you would want to have. Would it be x-ray vision, super strength, the ability to be invisible or travel through time... or something else?

SOUL FOOD:

- Psalm 44:21
- Psalm 139
- Hebrews 4:13

DADDY BRAINS

"Dad, I'm going to blow
in your ear..."
– Bethany, age 4

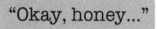
"Okay, honey..."

(blows in ear)

"Did it come out the other side?"

Have you ever known anyone who seemed like they just didn't have anything between their ears? Maybe they gave non-sensical answers, or didn't have a sweet clue what was going on.

I'll admit that was me in math class. My brains seemed to either fall asleep or fall right out whenever I was asked, what the area of a convex polygon or the root of an equation was. It certainly is very important to learn math, science, geography, and history, but more importantly God says to gain WISDOM. Perhaps you know a lot of facts, but they will do you no good without wisdom. Wisdom is being able to use those facts properly. Wisdom is applied knowledge.

Maybe mom and dad have heard this saying before: "Knowledge is knowing a tomato is a fruit. Wisdom is not putting it in a fruit salad!" (Yuk!) Or, knowledge is calculating how many miles you are about to hike, but wisdom is bringing along enough water to keep you going. Do you see the difference now? We can learn a lot from our teachers, Pastors and parents, but who we can learn the most from is our Heavenly Father. *He's* got some *really* big daddy brains!

Proverbs is a book of the Bible that I have always loved. King Solomon, the writer of Proverbs, was a man full of wisdom. He shares many things he has learned from God, and from living a long life. You would be wise to listen to the lessons in that book and apply them to your own life. And also listen to your parents, because they've been around the block a few times! But it isn't just the book of Proverbs, the entire Bible is full of wisdom.

Living for and following Jesus requires faith, but God gives us faith through reading the Bible. I find that God's ways simply make a lot of sense! As you continue to learn from His word, I'm sure you will find that same thing out too!

GET 'EM TALKING:

Here are some "fun facts". Talk about ways that you can use this information wisely!

- The medical term for bad breath is *Halitosis*.

- The standard store-bought "healthy" muffin has about 800 calories of sugar and fat – as much as maybe 2 donuts!

- *Carpal Tunnel syndrome* is numbness, tingling, and pain in the hand, wrist, and arm area, caused by repetitive over-use of electronic devices such as video game controllers and iPhones. Teenagers and children are developing carpal tunnel younger and younger each year.

SOUL FOOD:

- Proverbs 1:7
- Proverbs 2: 6-7
- Proverbs 15:33
- Proverbs 4

HEAVENLY PERFECTION

> "The old people...they were all just... SO UGLY!!"
>
> – Keaton, age 6

One of Keaton's many talents is singing like a bird – so much so, that a song he sang lead vocal on, won the Covenant Award's Canadian Children's song of the year in 2017! His first experience singing with a kid's choir was also his first experience in a nursing home. About 40 kids caroled for the seniors at Christmas time. It was a delight! All the kids did a great job and had a fun time. I thought Keaton was enjoying himself too, but on the car ride home he let out a big sigh, and his face took on a look of concern. When I asked him what was wrong, he hesitantly said to me, "I don't want to sound mean, and please don't get me in trouble, but mom, the old people...they were all just SO UGLY!!!"

I had to chuckle a little, and told him it was ok. He wasn't in trouble. I thanked him though, that he waited until we were in the car to express his thoughts! I hadn't thought about how overwhelming it might be for him to walk into a room of ninety-year-olds...complete with walkers, wheelchairs, bad coughs, and breathing tubes. And worse – double chins and very hairy ears! He hadn't seen anything like it before!

In the car ride home, we talked about the fact that in this life, our body is not perfect. It ages and wears out on us. And yes, things can get ugly! I assured him that it is only our temporary dwelling though. The Bible says that when we get to Heaven, we will finally be perfect! No more aches and pains, and no more sagging skin and balding heads. (All the grandmas and grandpas said a big AMEN!) I am so very glad that there will be a day when we do not have to worry about sickness or sadness, or our eyes and ears not functioning as they should. The Bible tells us that we'll have "heavenly bodies" and that we will be "buried in brokenness, but raised in glory, buried in weakness, but raised in strength"! The best part will be that we will live with Jesus forever! If you've ever wondered about Heaven, know that it's ALL GOOD!

GET 'EM TALKING:

- Brainstorm some ways that you can help the elderly people in your life, whose bodies are wearing out on them. Perhaps you could help shovel their driveway if they don't have as much "steam in their engine" as you. Or maybe you could listen to them tell stories about when they were young and energetic like you. I know they'd love that! What else could you do!?

SOUL FOOD:

- 2 Corinthians 5:1-5

SILVER CONVERTIBLES

"Mommy, why do all the people who drive convertibles have silver hair?"

– Neighbor, Keri, age 7

My next door neighbor is THE BEST. We love hanging out together and chatting up a storm. While sitting together, watching marching bands, fire trucks and Convertibles roll by at our Village's Memorial Day Parade, my neighbor told me the funniest story. Her sweet daughter, Keri, asked her a puzzling question during a previous parade: "Mommy, why do all people who drive Convertibles have silver hair?" My neighbor laughed and replied, "Because by the time parents pay for their kid's braces, college, and weddings, they can finally afford it!"

I agree that kids don't come cheap! As a mom I sometimes feel guilty buying anything for myself, but if it's for my kids, I'll slap down some cash faster than a toupee flies off a head in a hurricane! I've been needing a few pairs of socks and pajama pants, but I'd wear holes in my socks any day if it meant that my boys could join the baseball league.

Remember Keri's idea that Cadillacs come to people with silver hair? Well, good things come to all of us, and come through many different ways. We may need to wait for them or work hard for them. It is important to know that we must wait for some good things in life; it is also important to WORK for those things. What are some things you want to work towards, and achieve before your hair is...ahem...SILVER? Convertibles are cool, but I know that God has WAY cooler things in store for you and your family.

GET 'EM TALKING:

- Discuss the things that you hope to achieve both short-term and long-term (as individuals and a family), and how you are going to achieve them. Write down your answers. Pray and commit those things to God. Ask him to help you achieve your dreams.

SOUL FOOD:

- Galatians 6:9
- Romans 8:25 and 12:11-12
- Colossians 3:23-24
- Proverbs 10:4
- Proverbs 28:19

I STOLE THE COOKIE FROM THE COOKIE JAR

> "Jesus was in the kitchen.
> He told me I could have a cookie."
>
> – Case, age 3 [1]

There's nothing better or more irresistible than the smell of freshly baked chocolate chip cookies. They can be REALLY hard to resist, especially when they are still warm from the oven. Even adults have a hard time with that. The struggle is real!

I've always called Braden my "sous chef". He loves helping me in the kitchen while I'm baking. The fact that he gets to lick the spoon and test out a treat upon it's exit from the oven are great motivators. I love being with my little helper, and I don't mind letting him be my taste tester – as long as it's under my terms. Braden knows that if he tries to sneak a finger in the bowl before I allow it, he'll be told to exit the kitchen immediately. He must not give in to his temptation.

Temptation isn't just in the kitchen. It's all around us...*all* the time. Cookies aren't the only thing that tempt us: friends, books, TV shows, our brothers and sisters.

---

(1) http://www.huffingtonpost.com/entry/hilarious-and-oddly-insightful-quotes-from-kids_us_56bdef80e4b08ffac124b744

There will always be something or someone luring you in. Does Jesus want to keep fun things from you to punish you or make your life miserable?? NO!! In fact, Jesus wants your life not to be filled just with good things, but He wants the absolute *best* things for you. That is why He's put limits and boundaries on some things, so that we do not get hurt.

I know that sometimes it can feel like God, pastors, teachers, or your parents aren't allowing you to do, watch, read, or eat pleasurable things. Ultimately, we have to trust and obey our authorities. Sometimes too much of a good thing can actually be bad. God has laid out a set of rules and boundaries in the Bible to help keep us from harm. If we disobey those things, we are sinning against Him.

When you know that you have given into temptation and disobeyed, the best thing that you can do is simply CONFESS. Satan, our enemy, wants you to keep your sins a secret. He hates it when we obey and follow God's rules. But, God loves us so much and wants to keep us safe. The Bible says that when we confess (tell someone and admit our wrong behavior), God understands. He will forgive us, and He will send His Holy Spirit to help us not sin again. Sin not only hurts God, but it will eventually hurt you as well. That is why I know that God would never tell you to disobey. We can never hide our sin from God anyway, so when you know that you've done something wrong, don't try to cover it up. Instead, fess up and move on! So, the next time your mom asks, "who stole the cookie from the cookie jar!?" - if it was you - tell the truth!

GET 'EM TALKING:

We've just been talking about the importance of TRUTH telling, especially when we mess up. Now, let's have a little fun. I've got some DARES for you! I DARE you to have some fun doing these during your meal! Parents, please forgive me for all the craziness that's about to ensue!

- Eat a spoonful of mustard

- Hold an ice cube in your hand tight for 30 seconds.

- Sing the Alphabet song backwards.

- Keep a straight face while the person to the right of you tries to make you laugh

- Try to lick the tip of your elbow.

SOUL FOOD:

- James 5:16
- Proverbs 28:13
- 1 John 1:9
- Luke 12:2
- Hebrews 2:18

MONKEY SEE, MONKEY DO

Mom: "Are you going to play nice with the other kids?"

"Are you going to play nice with the other moms?"
– Layla, age 4 [1]

Kids sure do keep parents on their toes, don't they!? Raising kids is challenging in many ways, but one of the most thought-provoking things is when THEY challenge YOU! As my kids have grown a bit older, THEY are the ones keeping ME accountable, making sure that I'm living the way that I expect them to live as well. We have been kept accountable on many occasions, hearing things like: "Mom, shouldn't you put that grocery cart back where it belongs?", or "Dad, you've got too much road rage!", or "Mom and dad, can you stop looking at your phones and actually watch my game!?" Embarrassing and shameful, but true.

Kids have got eyes in the backs of their heads too, and they catch *every*thing. You're smarter than you let on, aren't you, kiddos!? So, parents, we will never be

---

(1) http://www.huffingtonpost.com/entry/hilarious-and-oddly-insightful-quotes-from-kids_us_56bdef80e4b08ffac124b744

perfect, but we must strive to have our actions line up with our words. We must minimize the "do as I say...not as I do" moments. And, we must model Christ-likeness consistently, because the kiddos are watching.

Kids, remember that your parents aren't perfect. They make mistakes. But they love you and want the best for you. The fact that they are reading this book with you is proof of that! Be understanding, forgiving, and listen to your parents! And, realize that one day you might be a parent too!

GET 'EM TALKING:

- Everyone take turns looking up the Soul Food scripture verses. Explain each verse, and why it is important to do what you say and not be hypocritical. What are the repercussions of not setting a good example?

SOUL FOOD:

- James 4:17
- 1 John 4:20
- Hebrews 13:7
- 1 Timothy 4:12
- Matthew 5:16

22
DREAM MAKER

"Baseball is just a field of
broken dreams..."
– Braden, age 4

It was a sunny and warm February day; extremely unusual for Buffalo, NY. Keaton, who dreams of being an MLB baseball player, relentlessly begged his younger brother to join him in the back yard to play catch. Braden wasn't quite as enthusiastic about the thought. He laid across our sunroom chair, gazing out the window, and responded with a "NO!" for the thirteenth time. When Keaton pleaded for an explanation, Braden answered with: "Baseball is just a field of broken dreams." It sounded so cute and funny coming from a four-year-old (as if he'd experienced such heartache before). Clearly, Braden had picked up this line from somewhere else, and was just repeating what he'd heard. Braden has never suffered through the pain of broken dreams, other than his ice cream falling off it's cone, or not getting his favorite green cup at dinner time. But, as he gets older, he will actually have bigger, more meaningful dreams that he hopes will come true – which I hope and pray *will* come true.

It is hard when things don't go according to plan. It is difficult to lose something you hoped would be yours. God understands when we are let down by this world. While we are living here on Earth, things and people will never be perfect, not even close! It is inevitable that things will not always go our way, and sometimes we will fail. But, I want to tell you that *God* will *never* fail you! God will *never* let you down. God will always turn the bad things that happen into good. That's His specialty! Don't give up, because God has awesome things in store for you! God has even bigger dreams for you than you have for yourself, and He will help you achieve them!

GET 'EM TALKING:

- What are some dreams you and your family have? Do you think that they are God's dreams for you too!? Be encouraged by these four verses below. They are some of my favorites.

SOUL FOOD:

- Jeremiah 29:11
- Psalm 37:4
- Proverbs 3:5-6
- Romans 8:28

THE BEST THINGS IN LIFE ARE FREE

"Mom, can we go to the store to
buy something with my
invisible money?"

– Braden, age 4

Sadly, in this life most things don't come free, and in a
lot of cases, they don't come cheap either! It seems
crazy that we have to spend money to park our car, throw
our garbage away, and even have clean running water. I
asked people on social media what they hate paying for,
and I heard things like: road tolls, air for their tires, and
other people's mistakes! It's just how life goes. (Sorry
kids, if I've unleashed some rage in your parents... Now
parents, take a big deep breath, in and out...)

I have some really great news. There are a few things in
life that are guaranteed to be received freely, with no
strings attached. God's love, His forgiveness, and the gift
of salvation are entirely FREE! We don't have to spend
hours of overtime, our blood sweat and tears, not even
one shiny penny on the BEST things that life has to offer.
God gives us *so* many free blessings on top of His love and
forgiveness, but even if this was all He offered, it would
be more than enough.

You don't need to earn or repay God's love. Nothing we
can do could ever repay what God has done for us. He's
completely cancelled our debt! Parents, that's one less
credit card you have to worry about! God doesn't need

anything from us. He owns everything in this world. It's ALL His. All He asks in return is our gratitude.

Get 'em talking:

- Starting oldest to youngest, say two things you are THANKFUL to God for.

Soul Food:

- Ephesians 2: 4-5, 8-9;
- Psalm 50:7-15

NOT ALL JOKES ARE FUNNY

(While watching Veggie Tales together...)

Me: "My favorite is Jr. Asparagus, because he's a cute little boy like you."

"My favorite is Bob the Tomato, because he's big and round like YOU!"

– Keaton, age 3

Unfortunately, many of Keaton's adorable quotes are at my expense. Yet I really don't mind! I know he probably didn't really know what he was saying. (At least I HOPE he didn't!) Throughout this book, we've talked a lot about the words that we speak – because words are VERY powerful!

What I want to focus on today is what can happen when we joke around with our words. Keaton was goofing around when he called me "big and round". In our case, it was harmless and funny, and it gave me a laugh. But joking isn't *always* harmless. We need to be careful with our words when we make jokes about people. Even if we think we're being funny and that everyone else, including the person we're joking about, laughs. Perhaps that person isn't laughing on the inside.

Be careful that you don't hurt others when you joke around. When you insult someone, disguising it as a joke, it is still an insult. Proverbs 26:18-19 says that saying something mean about someone, even if it is in a playful manner, is like hurling a flaming arrow at them. We all know a flaming arrow would hurt "like the dickens", as my Grandma would say. "Wise cracks" are really not all that wise. So, the next time you want to tease or poke fun at someone, be certain that the other person will actually enjoy your sense of fun!

GET 'EM TALKING:

Describe how these jokes could actually hurt someone's feelings:

- "Susan's nose is as long as an elephant's trunk! You could slide right down it! Haha!"

- "It took Derek three times as long to run that race as me. I finished, took a bath, made a lasagna and ate some, while I was waiting for him at the finish line. Lol!"

- "Veronica's mom forgets to pick her up from basketball practice as much as Veronica misses the basket when she shoots. Bahahah!"

SOUL FOOD:

- Proverbs 26:18-19

GOD DOESN'T MAKE MISTAKES

> "Dear God, did you mean for a giraffe to look like that, or was it an accident?"
>
> – a curious toddler [1]

Freckles, brown skin, piercing blue eyes, thick strong legs, curly red hair, are features that make people unique. Characteristics like being adventurous, fearless, or charming make people special. Maybe you've wondered if God got it right when He made you. Have you ever felt different from others? Do you ever wish you could change something about yourself? Have you ever wished you could be someone else? Well, if you have, you're not alone! Most of us have felt "uncomfortable in our own skin", especially as we are growing up and learning about ourselves. That is very normal. But, I want you to know that how you FEEL about yourself isn't always what is TRUE about you. We need to believe what God says about us, and not what others say, or what we think. Sometimes we can get it all wrong.

Check out these unique facts out about a giraffe. I don't think God got it wrong. It's amazing!

- A giraffe's lungs can hold 12 gallons (55 liters) of air!

---

(1) https://www.thesun.co.uk/archives/news/717692/kids-send-hilarious-letters-to-god

- No two giraffe spots are exactly alike. Each one is unique!

- Giraffes use their powerful necks to fight each other, and their hooves to defend themselves. They can kill a lion with their kick!

Maybe you're wishing you didn't have those long, lanky arms, or that quiet, less assertive personality, but I have a hunch that God created you exactly that way for a very good reason! You are made just the way you are with lots of care, and for a very important purpose! If you don't believe me, read Psalm 139:13-18. You will find out that you are "fearfully and wonderfully made"! You are unique. Yes, you are special! You are definitely not an accident!

GET 'EM TALKING:

- Put all the names of your family in a hat. Then take turns pulling out names. Tell the person you pick, one thing that God made wonderfully about them.

SOUL FOOD:

- Psalm 139:13-18

LOCK 'EM UP!

(After Dan made a cheesy "dad joke")

> "Dad, you need to lock your jokes up in jail!"
> — Braden, age 4

What harmful habits or behaviors do YOU need to "lock up in jail", or keep from happening again? What things in your life would you be better off without?

My boys' dad has a habit of telling cheesy jokes. It's true. "Dad humor" may make kids' eyes roll, but it is really quite harmless. Some habits, though, can be harmful. What things in your life do you have a habit of doing that could be harmful? Do you have any thought patterns, negative language, or destructive behaviors that would be better off put in prison? Maybe there are things you do from time to time that you know are wrong. Even one-time sins will become habitual and can harm us if we don't lock them up!

The way to lock sin up in jail is to EXPOSE it! A criminal must first be found before the police can toss them in their cruiser and keep them from doing any more wrong. In the same way, when we bring our darkness into the light, we trap it and keep it from running rampant and ruling our lives. The best way to stop our sin from growing is to shine God's spotlight on it. When we confess our sin to others, and to God, we handcuff all the bad stuff. God will take it and toss it into the slammer, and throw away the key!

GET 'EM TALKING:

- Parents, discuss with your children that God loves them and you love them unconditionally, and that their home is a safe place to make mistakes and learn from their mistakes. Encourage them to share the things they need help "locking up".

SOUL FOOD:

- Ephesians 5:11-13

MORE THAN A FEELING

> "Dear God, I bet it's very hard for you to love all of everybody in the whole world. There are only four people in our family, and I can never do it."
>
> – an honest child

Real life love is tough. Lasting love is even more tough. It's not like Hollywood movies and TV shows present it to be. Love takes commitment and a lot of hard work! It is more than just how we feel. Some days it can be really easy to love the people in our family, but many days it can be a challenge. Who *feels* like loving someone who is hogging the bathroom when you need to get ready? Who *feels* like loving someone who just yelled at you to take out the trash? Who *feels* loving towards someone with morning breath!? Who *feels* like loving someone who's refusing to eat the dinner it took you more than an hour to prepare? And yet, God tells us to love like *He* does – unconditionally – that means no matter what!

The Bible says that God's love for us is everlasting (Jeremiah 31:3), unfailing (Psalm 32:8), and enduring (Psalm 136:2). How does He do that!? It's true that as much as your parents love you, GOD loves you more than they ever could! That's even when He knows everything you've done: the good, the bad, and the ugly!

So, how do we love like God loves? Well, let's start with remembering how God has loved us. He didn't just tell us, but he showed us. He did something about it. He loved us so much that He GAVE. He sent his Son. He "put His money where His mouth was". Some of the parents out there might remember a song by a rap group DC Talk called "Love is a Verb". It reminds us that love isn't just a word we say, but it's also an action word. We must show our love by our actions, and our sacrifice.

When you're not *feeling* like showing love to your family, remember this phrase: "Right feelings follow right actions". If you aren't feeling loving to your spouse or to your mom and dad, guess what will help? Go and DO something loving for them anyway, and the feelings of love will eventually follow. That person will feel loved and you will feel more loving!

GET 'EM TALKING:

- Point out one thing that you can do this week that would show, or prove your love for every member of your family. Write it down, so you remember to do it! Then do it!

SOUL FOOD:

- John 3:16-17
- 1 Corinthians 13:4-7

GUT, GOOGLE, OR GOD?

> "One, two, three, four,
> five, six, seven.
> Eight, nine, ten...
> Twelve. Eleven."
> – a song Keaton wrote at age 3

Keaton is certainly a budding song writer. He's got the musicality and the rhyming part down, but just like his momma, he's no mathematician! The cute little tune he created the day he wrote this song was spot on. I wish you could have heard it. The lyrics? They were on point... until the very end. You'll have to look closely to see where he went wrong.

It's funny how kids think they know everything. I have had legitimate arguments with my four-year-old that a bird's grandpa is his friend from school. What!? And, he was *certain*.

It is not just kids. Adults can certainly be wrong too, even when they are certain about something. There are things in daily life that seem to make sense or feel right. It's that "gut feeling". But still, it can lead me astray. Google doesn't always have things right either. But, God always has it right. His wisdom is far beyond ours. I've heard it said that we can no more understand the complexity of God than the pancake we made for breakfast can understand the complexity of us (Donald Miller, Blue Like

Jazz). So, whatever we do, and whatever we think, it would be wise of us to check in with the smartest guy we know! And, how we do that is to open up the book that He's given us, and use it as our manual and roadmap for life!

GET 'EM TALKING:

- Think of a time that you thought you were right about something, but then it ended up being all wrong and going all wrong. Looking back, what would you have done differently to prevent going down the wrong way?

SOUL FOOD:

- Proverbs 16:25
- Isaiah 55:8-9

JESUS IS THE MAIN COURSE

"Mom, what's for dinner?"
— Keaton, age 8

"I already told you: grilled cheese and a veggie platter."

"No, I mean like, what's the MAIN course?"

Honest confession: some nights I just don't feel like cooking. There are many times that my kids don't get gourmet or even relatively nutritious food. Some nights when this mom just can't get her act together, it's Mini Wheats for supper. I try to give my family what they need every meal time, but sometimes I fail. I am very, very thankful that God NEVER fails us. He always offers us His best. He wants to give us the "main course" every time. We will never be unsatisfied when we eat His "daily bread" and drink His "living water".

In the Bible, Paul pleads with Christ's followers to take advantage of the spiritual nourishment that God offers to us. He knows that God's word will make us spiritual giants. All too often we settle for the "milk", or the basics of Christianity, rather than feasting on all that God has to offer us. How foolish! We will be weak and continually unsatisfied if we only nibble at God's table. But, when we dive in and feast on God's word, our spiritual muscles will grow, and we will be able to defeat our enemy and handle everything that life hurls our way!

GET 'EM TALKING:

- Go around the table and say what your favorite main dish is. I'm guessing for some of you, it will be grilled cheese!

SOUL FOOD:

- 1 Corinthians 3:2

GOD AND GREEN BEANS

> "Mom, I already ate my
> invisible vegetables."
>
> – Braden, age 4

It's so darling how little children believe they can actually fool their parents. (But kids, we're on to you!) Lately, Braden has been trying to convince me that he does the many things I ask, but that I just don't see them, because they are "invisible". Apparently, he washes his hands with invisible soap and water, and he brushes his teeth with an invisible toothbrush.

On several occasions Braden has sincerely tried to convince me that he had eaten tons of peas, green beans, and carrots, but that I couldn't see them because they were invisible. From the matter-of-fact look on his face, I think that he might even have believed himself. When I asked him what they tasted like, he answered straight-faced with "like candy". Silly me. I should have known that. I am pretty sure that Braden wishes that vegetables tasted like candy as much as I wished that I could buy things at the store with invisible money (see Devo # 23).

Regrettably, vegetables sometimes aren't as good as candy, but the more you eat them, the tastier they get. Your body craves what you feed it. So feed it things that are good for you! Now, I honestly would rather eat a plate full of roasted sweet potatoes over a bag of Sour Patch

Kids any day of the week! That's because I've taught my body to love REAL food. Eating REAL healthy foods and having *real* healthy habits will grow us *visible* muscles and, even better, it will give us *visible* energy to live for our very *real* God the way that He created us to live.

It's fun to eat junk food, and sometimes skip our daily health routines. However, we must be careful that it's not on a regular basis. Did you know that you are responsible to take care of the body that God blessed you with? Even though it is only our temporary home, God calls our bodies "His temple", or His house. If we are living with Him in our hearts, our bodies are what we use to serve Him and what we use to point others to Him. If we are misusing our bodies, being destructive to them, or denying them the things that they need, we aren't honoring God and we won't be able to live for Him the way we should.

Even though God seems "invisible", it is important to honor him every way that we can – sometimes that means eating *real* green beans!

GET 'EM TALKING:

- What are some ways we can take care of our bodies, our "temples"? What are some behaviors whereby we abuse or harm them?

SOUL FOOD:

- 1 Corinthians 6:19-20
- 1 Corinthians 10:31

BEST DECISION EVER!

> "Today I talked to God! I asked
> Him to come live inside my heart!"
>
> – Keaton, age 4

Decisions, decisions. Life is FULL of decisions. By the time you head out for work or school, you've decided whether to hit "snooze" on the alarm for a few more cozy minutes with your eyes closed, you've chosen between Raisin Bran or Captain Crunch, and whether to wear the blue sweater or the black one. Studies show that kids make around 3,000 decisions in a single day. Adults make upwards of 35,000 decisions a day. Most decisions you make aren't really significant in the grand scheme of things, but some decisions we make are crucial ones and will affect our entire lives.

Some of the most important decisions we make are who our friends will be, where we will go to school, what job we choose, and who we decide to marry. These types of decisions shape our lives. However, the most impactful decision you will EVER make is whether you choose to believe in and follow God, and believe in His son, Jesus, and the path He prepared for you.

A well-known Christian author, A.W. Tozer writes: "What comes into our minds when we think about God is the most important thing about us." That may seem like an overstatement at first, but when you stop to think about it, who we choose to believe God is, will dictate the entire way we live our lives. If we think that He is some absentee landlord who doesn't care about the details of our life, we won't put our trust in Him. If we think that He is angry, strict, and unjust, we will run away from Him. But, if we choose to believe by faith that God is who He says He is, we will come running to Him.

I really hope that you take the time to read the "Soul Food" verses today, so that you can get a glimpse of who God is. Choosing to believe Him, follow Him, and live with Him guiding your heart is THE best decision you will ever make!

GET 'EM TALKING:

Here's a fun game full of decisions for you to play while you're munching on your food tonight. It's called "Would You Rather". Take turns asking the questions to each other and see how well you know one other. Guess what each family member will say.

WOULD YOU RATHER...

1. Go sky diving or scuba diving?
2. Eat a big bowl of worms, or a big bowl of dirt?
3. Live without the internet or without running water?
4. Be transported for a day to the past or to the future?
5. Eat a donut or ice cream?
6. Be a famous actor or a famous athlete?
7. Have spinach stuck in your teeth, or a booger hanging out of your nose?
8. Read a fiction book or non-fiction book?
9. Live in a castle or on a yacht?
10. Play a sport or play video games?

Prayer:

If you are ready to accept Jesus as your Savior

"Dear God, I believe in you. I believe in your son, Jesus, and that He gave His life so that I could live forever with you. God, please come into my heart. Please forgive the wrong things I have done and help me to follow you. I choose to believe that your way is the best way. I want to live forever with you in Heaven. Thank you for loving me and saving me. Amen."

If you are not ready to honestly say the above prayer yet, read through these Bible verses, and then ask God to help you believe and to make Himself real to you.

Soul Food:

- John 3:16
- Romans 10:9
- Romans 8:38-39
- Romans 5:8
- Ephesians 2:4-5

Easy, Family-Friendly, Nourishing Recipes

Here are some of the Macaulay's easy favorite go-to kid friendly recipes that include mostly healthy ingredients, but are still yummy enough that there's not too much of a fight - or none at all, at the table.

As I'm sure it's the case at your house too, there is NEVER a fight here over desert (other than who gets the biggest piece!) Enjoy!

BREAKFAST

LIQUID REECE'S PIECES SMOOTHIE

- 3-4 C ice
- 2-3 C almond milk
  (as much as you need to blend smoothly)
- 2 Tbsp chocolate protein powder
- Half a banana
- 3 C baby spinach
- 2-4 Tbsp peanut butter (to liking)

The best green smoothie you'll ever taste - that is, if you like Reece's Pieces!

Blend all ingredients together in high powered mixer. Adjust ingredients according to your desired flavor intensity and ability to blend smoothly. Drink immediately - it won't keep for long.

DANIELLE'S EASY BANANA BREAD

- 3-4 ripe bananas
- 1/3 C melted butter (5 1/3 tbsp)
- 3/4 C granulated sugar
- 1 egg, beaten
- 1 tsp vanilla
- 1 tsp baking soda
- pinch of salt
- 1/8 C ground flax (optional)

This is my boy's all time favorite. It's mine too, because it's so easy and perfect for breakfast, snacks, bagged lunches and even dessert. A loaf never lasts 24 hrs in our home.

1 1/2 C all purpose flour (my fav combo is 1/2 C all purpose and 1 C whole wheat flour)

No need for a mixer! Simply preheat oven to 350 degrees F. In a lg bowl, mix the melted butter into the mashed bananas and then add sugar, egg and vanilla. Sprinkle baking soda and salt over the mixture and then add the flour (no need to sift either!). Incorporate.

Pour mixture into a buttered 4x8 inch loaf pan. I prefer one with a rounded edge. Bake 50 min - 1 hr until golden brown on top and baked fully through.

AUNT JOAN'S FRUIT MUFFINS

- 1 ½ cups all-purpose flour
  (I use whole wheat flour for ½ cup)
- 1 C white sugar
- 1 tsp. baking powder
- 1 tsp. baking soda
- 1 tsp. cinnamon
- ½ tsp. salt
- ¼ C wheat germ or ground flax (optional)
- 1 C grated carrot
- ¾ C blueberries
  (frozen are fine, and don't need to be thawed)
- 2 beaten eggs
- 2/3 C cooking oil (I use Crisco)
- ½ C crushed pineapple, including juice
- 1 tsp. vanilla
- ¼ C wheat bran

A tasty muffin packed with fruit AND veggies, amongst other things that keep your digestive system flowing!

Stir dry ingredients together. Stir in grated carrot and blueberries. Mix together wet ingredients, and combine with dry, stirring only until combined. Do not beat. Divide batter into 12 greased muffin cups. Sprinkle ½ teaspoon wheat bran over top of each muffin. Bake 20 minutes in 400 degree F oven.

Danielle's Chocolate Oatmeal Bake

- 1/4 C rolled oats
- 2 Tbsp wheat bran
- 2 Tbsp whole wheat flour
- 1 Tbsp shredded coconut
- 1 tsp cacao powder
- 1/4 tsp baking powder
- pinch of salt
- 1/2 C unsweetened almond milk
- 1 Tbsp pure maple syrup
- 1/8 tsp almond extract
- 1/4 C dark chocolate chips

Our family eats food like this recipe, bowls of oatmeal with apples, eggs, smoothies etc., MUCH more than the sugary cereals we all grew up on. With some simple planning, you can give your kiddos a hearty and healthy breakfast they love that will keep them going all day.

Preheat oven to 375 degrees F and lightly coat an individual sized oven-safe ramekin. This can be made individually, or you may double or quadruple the recipe, depending on how many mouths you have to feed. Grease ramekins with coconut oil. In a medium-sized bowl, combine dry ingredients. Add almond milk, maple syrup, almond extract and chocolate chips, mixing until well combined. Transfer dough to your greased ramekin, topping with a few chocolate chips if desired. Bake for 20-25 minutes, depending on desired consistency.

Sausage, Pepper and Egg Wraps

- 4 whole wheat tortilla wraps
- 8 large eggs
- 1/4 C diced peppers of choice
- 1/8 C finely diced onion
- 4 breakfast sausage patties
- grated cheese of your choice
- A few shakes of hot sauce (if you like things spicy)

So satisfying and energy supplying, and these are great to cook, wrap up, and bring with you if you're on the run. Try these for a winning dinner too!

Saute peppers and onions together, and then scramble the eggs in with the peppers. Cook and dice the sausage patties and toss in the egg/pepper mixture. Divide mixture evenly in each wrap, and then top with the cheese. Wrap up, and go!

SNACK

CACAO YOGURT DIP
(best with berries!)

This dip is a result of some experimenting with healthier ingredients, but a yummy taste. Often, I'll put these ingredients in a bowl, mix in some berries, cashews or almonds, chia seeds, cacao nibs, or whatever I can find in my pantry for a healthy, but sweet lunch too.

Ingredients:

- 1 C plain greek yogurt
- 1 Tbsp cacao
- 2 1/2 tsp pure maple syrup

DARK CHOCOLATE BARK

- 1 12oz pkg dark chocolate chips
- dried cherries or cranberries
- chopped whole raw almonds
- chopped raw cashews
- chia seeds
- pumpkin seeds

Pair the healthiest "trail mix" ingredients with some antioxidant packed dark chocolate for the win! Your kids will not say no. The best part: this snack can be prepared in all of 3 minutes.

Melt chocolate carefully over a double boiler. Pour onto parchment covered sheet pan and spread thin with a rubber spatula. Sprinkle chocolate with your favorite ingredients (mine are listed above, but feel free to try other dried fruits, nuts and seeds). Put a plastic baggie on your hand, and then gently press the toppings into the chocolate.

Refrigerate at least 1 hr, and then peel parchment off the bottom and begin to break into pieces. Store in airtight container in the fridge.

DATE HONEY
(eat with crisp and crunchy apples!)

Ingredients:
- 1 C pitted fresh medjool dates
- 1 C water
- 1/2 tsp cinnamon

My sister in law first introduced this recipe to me when we did the Daniel Fast. My youngest asks for it even when we're not cutting our dairy, sugar or carbs.

Pour pitted dates into a small pot. Fill pot with the water and make sure all dates are submerged. Bring water to a boil over high heat then reduce to low, simmering 15-30 min, or until the dates are very soft and broken down.

Remove pot from heat and cool slightly. Pour dates and water into a food processor or blender, add cinnamon and blend until smooth. Store in a sealed container in the fridge.

Danielle's Guacamole

(eat with salty tortilla chips or veggie sticks)

- 3 ripe avocados, with pits removed, diced into big chunks
- 1/2 a lg tomato, seeded and diced
- 1/4 C finely diced onion - red is my favorite, but any variety will do
- 1/8 - 1/4 C freshly squeezed lime juice
- 1/4 C chopped fresh cilantro
- 1 lg minced garlic clove
- 1 - 1 1/2 tsp salt

My hubby's all time fav snack. Mix ingredients together in a bowl, being careful to keep chunks intact.

These measurements are a starting place. Feel free to play around and add everything to taste - if you prefer a strong garlic taste, then go for it. If you like a good zing, add more lime juice or cilantro. You may also need more salt, depending on the type of chip you use for scooping.

"CHOCOLATE" MINT ENERGY BITES

- 1 C walnuts
- 1 C pitted Medjool dates
- 1/3 C cacao powder
- 2 Tbsp almond milk
- 1-1 1/2 tsp peppermint extract
- 1 C shredded sweetened coconut for rolling

Another guilt free staple snack at the Macaulay house. Are you ready to get your hands dirty?! Don't worry - no one but you will know if you lick them clean afterwards.

Pulse walnuts in food processor. Add dates and pulse to incorporate well. I prefer using dates that have not been pre pitted. I find that when I pit them myself, they are much more fresh and will incorporate easily. Add cacao, peppermint extract and almond milk and mix until well combined.

Refrigerate for about a half hour to set. Form into balls by rolling about a tablespoon of the mixture between the palms of your hands. Place coconut into shallow bowl and roll balls in coconut to coat. May be placed in fridge for 1-2 weeks or in freezer for several months.

http://livingwellmom.com/2015/11/chocolate-mint-balls/

LUNCH

SUGAR FREE CHIA SEED JAM
(FOR PB &J'S)

- 2 C frozen berries
- 1-2 Tbsp honey or agave (to taste)
- 1-2 Tbsp fresh lemon juice (to taste)
- 2 Tbsp chia seeds

Bagged lunches are a must. It can be tricky to keep the sugar down in all the packaged and convenience foods we toss in those bags. This fast and easy jam recipe is one great way I've found to cut the sugar!

Place all ingredients in a pot on med-low heat. As fruit begins to cook, mash together and incorporate all ingredients well until fully mashed and fully cooked together. Let cool.

Taste your jam to make sure it has reached your desired sweetness/tartness and adjust accordingly. Store in an airtight container in fridge up to 2 weeks (off the books, I've had it in the fridge even longer and it's still good. I always use it up before it has a chance to go bad).

It's that simple!

DANIELLE'S ROASTED TOMATO SOUP WITH GRILLED CHEESE CROUTONS

- 10 roma tomatoes, cut in half lengthwise
- 3 Tbsp extra virgin olive oil
- 1 tsp salt
- 1/2 tsp pepper
- 1 lg yellow onion, chopped
- 4 garlic cloves, minced
- 2 tbsp olive oil
- 1 Tbsp butter
- 1 lg (28 oz) can crushed tomatoes
- 1 quart (32 oz) chicken or vegetable stock
- 1/2 C fresh basil leaves, julienned

Even my youngest asks for this soup regularly. I hope your kiddos will love it too!

Toss Tomatoes in olive oil, s&p in a lg bowl, and then lay on baking sheet, skin side down. Roast in 400 degree F oven for 40 min.

Sautee onion and garlic in olive oil and butter on med heat until translucent (add onion first, and then garlic after a minute or two).

When onion and garlic are ready, add the crushed tomato, stock, basil and the roasted tomatoes with all their pan juices. Bring to a boil, and then simmer on low about a half hour.

Puree in blender or with hand held blender until desired texture is achieved. Season with more salt and pepper to taste. I prefer my soup a bit chunky and rustic, served with grilled cheese croutons.

*Grilled cheese croutons: Our all time fav way to do grilled cheese is with colby jack cheese (use cheese of your choice, but none of that processed junk!) and whole wheat country bread, grilled on our panini grill. I then dice into crouton sized cubes and pile on top of soup.

I like to save a few pieces to pop into my mouth separately. Trust me, when I say that this is a far superior way to eat this classic winter comfort food!

VEGGIE PANCAKES

- 2 yukon gold potatoes, washed and grated
- 2 carrots, peeled and grated
- 1 zucchini, washed and grated
- 1 yellow squash, washed and grated
- 4 lg eggs
- 1/2 C whole wheat flour (maybe a bit more, depending on moisture level)
- 1 tsp salt
- sour cream or plain greek yogurt and chopped scallions for garnish

This is a tasty way to fool the kids into eating more veggies. They'll never know how many are packed into these pancakes.

Mix all vegetables together in a bowl. Squeeze moisture out of shavings with a clean kitchen towel and then return to bowl. Mix in remaining ingredients.

Using a half cup scoop, drop mounds onto a buttered skillet on med heat. Press down to flatten into a pancake.

When one side is browned, flip and cook until other side is golden brown. Garnish, season with more salt to taste and serve immediately.

DINNER

Danielle's Sweet Carrot Salad

- 1/2 lb carrots, peeled, ends cut, grated largely
- 1/2 C golden raisins
- 1/2 C diced pineapple
- 2 Tbsp freshly squeezed lemon juice
- 1/4 C good mayo
- 3 Tbsp white sugar

Carrots are sweet already, but when you pair them with pineapple and this sweet dressing, your kids will think they are eating candy! Toss the first 3 ingredients in a bowl, and then whisk the last 3 ingredients in a separate bowl.

Mix together and refrigerate at least 3 hrs before serving.

TERRI'S CHILI

- 1 1/2 - 2 lbs ground beef
- 1 chopped onion
- 1 green pepper

Brown these together, then add:

- 1 lg (28 oz) can crushed tomatoes
- 1 can rinsed kidney beans
- 1 Tbsp cider vinegar
- 1 Tbsp sugar
- 1 stalk chopped celery
- 1 C tomato juice
- 1 tsp cayenne pepper
- 1-4 dashes Frank's hot sauce (to liking)
- 1-2 Tbsp chili powder (to liking)
- 1 tsp salt
- black pepper to taste

I don't think I could count the number of times I've made this. Each winter this is a hit with the whole family, and a great way to get those veggies into them without them complaining one bit!

Simmer about 2 hrs and serve with tortilla chips, grated cheddar, sour cream (I substitute with plain greek yogurt) and chopped scallions for garnish.

*When watching my waist line, I like to cut the beef in half and replace with 1 pound of ground turkey. I also often add in a red and yellow pepper and diced tomato as well, to amp up the nutrition!

PAM'S CLEAN MEXICAN SALAD

Dressing:

- 1/4 C olive oil
- 1/4 C white balsamic vinegar
- juice from one lime
- rind of one lime
- 2 minced garlic cloves
- 1/4 tsp sea salt
- 1 Tbsp minced cilantro

Salad:

- 1 can corn
- 1 head romain lettuce
- 1/2 C baby tomatoes
- 1 can black beans
- 1 diced avocado
- 1 C broken tortilla chips

Directions:

This is one of our favorite easy summer salads. Even though this is a "clean" recipe, you definitely won't feel like you're missing out. You'll get a thumbs up from the kids because there's chips in the salad!

Mix all dressing ingredients together and pour over the salad or serve it on the side of the salad.

Toss all salad ingredients together.

Be sure to wash and throughly dry the corn and black beans or else it will make your salad soggy!

https://cleanlifehappywife.wordpress.com/2015/05/02/
clean-mexican-salad-with-lime-dressing/

EASY HOME MADE BREADED CHICKEN
(BETTER THAN THE FROZEN STUFF)

- 3-4 slices whole wheat bread (fresh or stale)
- 1/8 C grated parmesan cheese
- 1/4 tsp pepper
- 1/4 tsp salt
- 1/2 Tbsp dried parsley

(mix these ingredients together in food processor)

- 6 thin chicken strips or 4 lg thinly sliced breasts
- 2-3 eggs, depending on size
- 1/2 C flour of your choice

My boys often refuse to eat chicken unless it's breaded, but most of the time I refuse to buy the frozen stuff. This is my solution.

Put flour, eggs, and mixed breading mixture separately in three different shallow soup bowls. Season chicken with salt and pepper. Dredge chicken first through the flour, then egg and finally breading.

Fry in pan with butter and oil until golden brown and fully cooked through.

2 INGREDIENT PANCAKES FOR DINNER
(WITH 2 EXTRAS)

- 4 ripe Bananas
- 4 lg eggs
- 1/4 tsp baking powder (optional)
- 1/2 tsp cinnamon (optional, but yummier)

Blend ingredients together in a blender and cook just like regular pancakes. That's it!

Perfect if you're gluten or dairy free. So easy and so much better for you than regular pancakes. You're also almost always guaranteed to have the ingredients on hand.

DESSERT

DANIELLE'S CHOCOLATE CHIP COOKIES

- 2/3 C unsalted butter (10 tbsp), melted
- 2 C lightly packed brown sugar
- 2 eggs
- 2 Tbsp hot water
- 2 3/4 C all purpose flour
- 1 tsp baking powder
- 1 tsp baking soda
- 1/4 tsp salt
- 2 C semi sweet chocolate chips

Who can resist a chocolate chip cookie hot off the press? Not me! Not anyone in our family!

Preheat oven to 375 degrees F. Combine melted butter, brown sugar, eggs and hot water. Mix well (add sugar and eggs together first before the hot water and butter, to prevent the eggs from scrambling).

Stir in remaining ingredients, adding the chocolate chips last. Drop by tablespoonfuls onto an ungreased cookie sheet. Press down firmly to flatten quite a bit.

This recipe makes about 3 pans of cookies. Feel free to store extra dough in airtight container and place in fridge for your next craving. It will last many weeks that way.

Make sure you bring dough to room temp before baking. Do not put cookies in oven until it is fully preheated.

Bake exactly 9 minutes (all ovens vary, so pay attention - you may need to adjust accordingly).

They will look a bit underdone, but remove from oven anyway. Let cool on pan 10-15 minutes, and then transfer to wire rack to complete cooling process.

You must sneak at least one cookie hot off the press (the perks of being the baker!)

Dan's Apple Crisp

- 5-6 Apples (depending on size) of your favorite variety, peeled and cut into med-large slices
- 2-3 Tbsp granulated sugar
- 3/4 tsp cinnamon
- 1/2 tsp salt
- 1/2 C brown sugar
- 1/2 C rolled oats
- 1/3 C all purpose flour
- 4 Tbsp cold unsalted butter (1/2 stick) cut into small pieces, plus more for coating dish.

Heat oven to 350 degrees F and arrange rack to center position. Lightly coat an 8x8 inch glass baking dish with butter. Combine apple slices, granulated sugar, cinnamon and 1/4 teaspoon of the salt in a large bowl and toss together to coat apples. Place the mixture in dish and set aside.

Then, mix together the brown sugar, oats, flour and remaining salt until combined. Using your hands, blend in the butter pieces until small clumps form and butter is well incorporated. Sprinkle topping over the apple mixture and bake until topping is crispy golden brown and fruit is tender, about 50-60 min.

(Visit my blog page to hear the funny story behind this recipe frommilktomeat.com.)

Danielle's Birthday Oreo Cake

If you like chocolate mousse and Oreo combination...
beware! For an easier dessert, just make the chocolate
mousse.

Crust:
- 3 C chocolate wafer crumbs
- 9 Tbsp salted butter, melted

Mousse Filling:
- 2 3/4 C semi sweet chocolate
- 2 lg eggs
- 4 lg eggs, separated
- 2 C heavy cream
- 2 Tbsp sugar
- 1 tsp vanilla

Topping:
- 1 1/2 C heavy cream
- 2 Tbsp sugar
- 1 tsp vanilla

Crust:
Grind the chocolate wafers in a food processor. Place
them in a small bowl and add the melted butter. Press
the crumb mixture into a 10 inch springform pan,
covering the bottom and sides evenly. Refrigerate the
pan.

Mousse Filling:
Melt the chocolate in the top of a double boiler. Remove it from the heat and transfer the softened chocolate to a large bowl. Add the whole eggs and mix in well, using an electric mixer. Add the yolks and mix together. Scrape down the sides of the bowl and mix it again. In a separate bowl, whip the heavy cream until soft peaks form.
In another bowl, beat the egg whites until stiff. Fold the cream and egg whites into the chocolate mixture until it's completely incorporated. Pour the mixture into prepared crust and chill overnight or freeze for future use.

Topping:
Whip the heavy cream with the sugar and vanilla until stiff peaks form. Loosen the crust on all sides using a sharp knife and remove sides from springform pan. Cover cake with topping. Decorate top of cake with some crushed chocolate wafers, chocolate shavings, or a few raspberries.

DAN & BRADEN'S FAVORITE PEANUT BUTTER BARS - WITH CHOCOLATE GANACHE

- non-stick cooking spray
- 1 1/2 C confectioners sugar
- 1 1/2 C graham cracker crumbs
- 1 C creamy peanut butter
- salt
- 1 stick (8 Tbsp unsalted butter
- 8 oz semi sweet baking chocolate (2 boxes), cut in chunks
- 1 C heavy cream

Both my husband and my youngest son adore anything with chocolate and peanut butter involved. Me, not so much - EXCEPT this recipe. I can't get enough!

Coat bottom and sides of an 8x8 baking dish with spray. In a large bowl, stir to combine confectioners sugar, graham cracker crumbs, peanut butter, 1/8 teaspoon salt and melted butter. Press mixture into pan. Place chocolate and 1/8 teaspoon salt in a medium bowl.

Heat cream in a small sauce pan on low until bubbles start to form around the edges. Pour the cream over the chocolate and let sit for 1 minute, then whisk until completely melted together and smooth. Pour the ganache over the peanut butter mixture and refrigerate until chocolate is cooled and set, at least 1 hour.

Connie's Honeybun Cake

- 1 pkg yellow cake mix
- 3/4 C vegetable oil
- 4 eggs
- 1 (8 oz) container sour cream
- 1 C brown sugar
- 2 Tbsp milk
- 1/2 Tbsp vanilla
- 1 Tbsp ground cinnamon
- 1 C confectioners sugar

This is such an easy recipe but definitely a crowd pleaser - young and old!

Preheat oven to 325 degrees F. In a large mixing bowl, combine cake mix, oil, eggs and sour cream. Stir by hand about 50 strokes until most lumps are gone.

Pour half the batter into an un greased 9x13 glass dish. Combine brown sugar and cinnamon and sprinkle over batter in cake pan. Spoon other half of the batter into cake pan, covering the brown sugar mixture. Twirl cake batter with butter knife until it looks like a honeybun.

Bake in preheated oven for 40 minutes until toothpick comes out clean. In small bowl, whisk together icing sugar, milk and vanilla until smooth. Frost cake while still fairly hot. Let cool a bit, and serve warm.

ABOUT THE AUTHOR

Danielle Macaulay is the wife of worship leader and recording artist, Dan Macaulay and mom to adorable boys, Keaton and Braden. She enjoys writing, running, cooking, chatting it up with her friends (preferably at the spa), and watching a bit too much HGTV and Food Network. You can find nourishment for your body and soul at her popular blog spot "From Milk to Meat" (www.frommilktomeat.com)

Made in the USA
Columbia, SC
22 November 2017